The Essentia

F

500 & 600

Saloons/Sedans, Multipla, Giardiniera & 126
1955 to 1992

Your marque expert:
Malcolm Bobbitt

VELOCE PUBLISHING

THE PUBLISHER OF FINE AUTOMOTIVE BOOKS

www.veloce.co.uk

First published in February 2008 by Veloce Publishing Limited, Veloce House, Parkway Farm Business Park, Middle Farm Way, Poundbury, Dorchester, Dorset, DT1 3AR, England.
Reprinted November 2016 and June 2023. Fax 01305 268864/e-mail info@veloce.co.uk/web www.veloce.co.uk or www.velocebooks.com
ISBN: 978-1-787110-34-2 UPC: 6-36847-01034-8
Readers with ideas for automotive books, or books on other transport or related hobby subjects, are invited to write to the editorial director of Veloce Publishing at the above address.
British Library Cataloguing in Publication Data – A catalogue record for this book is available from the British Library.
Typesetting, design and page make-up all by Veloce Publishing Ltd on Apple Mac.
Printed and bound by CPI Group (UK) Ltd, Croydon, CR0 4YY.

Baby Fiats enjoy a history dating back to 1936 when Dante Giacosa's groundbreaking design became universally known as the Topolino. Post-war, the designer gave the world two more highly-innovative small cars, the first to appear in 1955, being the 600, which was of similar proportions to its predecessor but cleverly engineered as a rear-engined four-seater. Giacosa's innovativeness resulted in the versatile Multipla, the first true MPV which, in addition to seating six adults, could double as a camping car. Though the recipe was a triumph and Italians clamoured for the 600, there nevertheless remained a requirement for an even smaller car, one that was all the more simplistic in the idiom of the original Cinquecento. Giacosa knew exactly what his fellow Italians

The Nuova 500 had several guises, including the high performance Abarth 595.

wanted, and in 1957 created for them a new and charismatic 500. With its tiny footprint, miniscule rear-mounted air-cooled twin-cylinder engine with negligible running costs, room for two adults and a couple of children at a squeeze, the Nuova 500, accompanied by its 600 sibling, helped motorize Italy.

The 500 and 600 achieved cult status many years ago, courtesy of a loyal following that extended beyond their native Italy. These cars easily overrode social boundaries, especially when devotees of these minimal machines included some of the most famous motorsport personalities of the day. The demand for these iconic classics shows no sign of diminishing, and

When introduced in 1955, the Fiat 600 was Italy's favourite small car (Fiat).

this is where this book comes into its own. The intention is to guide the potential owner towards finding the right car to meet a budget, and by doing so explain how the purchaser should evaluate a particular vehicle. Step-by-step advice is given in every respect of a purchase, whether for a vehicle that is in concours condition or one that is eminently usable and which will provide much satisfaction. This book also caters for somebody happy buying a car that is in need of restoration, but whatever the reason for acquisition, there is in the following pages a wealth of information, from vital statistics to essential costing data, all of which will help make a confident purchase.

The intrinsic aspects of this guide are the key issues when considering a car that is offered for sale. Properly evaluating a vehicle will not only add to the experience of a purchase, but it will boost the pleasure of ownership.

Built on the 600 chassis, the multi-purpose Multipla set a trend. (Fiat)

Thanks
Peter Jones, Chairman of the Fiat Motor Club; Janet Westcott of the Fiat 500 Club; Jan di Carlo, ItalCorsa; Andrew Minney, Bill Wolf, William Imre, Steven Abbott, Ian Wallace, Colin Clarke, Attilio Savasi, Maria Cairnie, Martin Bates, Richard Dredge, Jamie Wright and Helen Reynolds.

Cover photograph supplied by *AutoItalia* magazine.

Essential Buyer's Guide™ currency
At the time of publication a BG unit of currency "●" equals approximately £1.00/US $1.24/Euro 1.15. Please adjust to suit current exchange rates.

Contents

Introduction & thanks
– the purpose of this book 3

1 Is it the right car for you?
– marriage guidance 6

2 Cost considerations
– affordable, or a money pit? 8

3 Living with a Fiat 500 or 600
– will you get along together? 10

4 Relative values
– which model for you? 12

5 Before you view
– be well informed 14

6 Inspection equipment
– these items will really help 16

7 Fifteen minute evaluation
– walk away or stay? 17

8 Key points
– where to look for problems 23

9 Serious evaluation
– 60 minutes for years of enjoyment .. 24

10 Auctions
– sold! Another way to buy your
  dream 42

11 Paperwork
– correct documentation is
  essential! 44

12 What's it worth to you?
– let your head rule your heart! 47

13 Do you really want to restore?
– it'll take longer and cost more
  than you think 48

14 Paint problems
– bad complexion, including
  dimples, pimples and bubbles 50

15 Problems due to lack of use
– just like their owners, baby Fiats
  need exercise! 52

16 The Community
– key people, organisations and
  companies in the Fiat world 54

17 Vital statistics
– essential data at your fingertips 56

Index 64

Tall and short drivers
These are tiny cars with narrow seats and small pedals. The forward-control Multipla has an odd driving position owing to the angle of the steering shaft. Seats adjust for forward and aft movement to allow the most comfortable driving position.

Weight of controls
Lightness gives the cars precise steering; gear changing requires practice. The clutch and brakes have a light feel.

Will it fit the garage?

	Length	Width
500 Nuova (All models)	9.74ft/2970mm	4.33ft/1320mm
500 Giardiniera	10.45ft/3185mm	4.34ft/1323mm
600	10.55ft/3215mm	4.53ft/1380mm
600D	10.81ft/3295mm	4.52ft/1378mm
600 Multipla	11.61ft/3540mm	4.76ft/1450mm
600D Multipla	11.63ft/3545mm	4.74ft/1445mm
126	10.02ft/3054mm	4.52ft/1377mm
126Bis	10.19ft/3107mm	4.52ft/1377mm

Interior space
The 500 and 126 have space enough for two adults and two children. The 600 will seat four adults, and the Multipla will seat six adults. Notwithstanding this, it is commonplace for baby Fiats to be seen packed to capacity with the entire family and their belongings.

Luggage capacity
Minimal! The front luggage compartment is limited in size, though extra baggage can be placed in the rear compartment if only two people occupy the car. The Multipla, however, is a load carrier, as long as six people are not accommodated! The 126Bis has, in addition to the front luggage compartment, a hatchback tailgate which gives access to storage space above the engine.

Running costs
Generally low, though some parts can be expensive, especially those for early models or rare derivatives.

Baby Fiats – such as this late model 500 pictured at Toronto – are particularly photogenic. (Bill Wolf)

Usability
Has to be driven at full speed to keep up with modern traffic. Can be intimidating when surrounded by large vehicles.

Parts availability and cost
Generally excellent, prices are mostly reasonable, but some tend to be expensive, particularly those for early cars.

Investment potential
Prices are stable due to the numbers of vehicles available. Rare variants are more expensive.

Foibles
Noisy and cramped.

Plus points
Fun; cult status; minimal fuel consumption; good club scene which gives access to parts suppliers and marque specialists.

Minus points
Vulnerable to rust, especially around front compartments, wings, wheelarches, sills and floorpan.

Alternatives
Bubblecars, Subaru 360, Honda N360 and the new Fiat 500 that was announced in July 2007.

The design of the Fiat 500 is ageless.
(Jamie Wright/Helen Reynolds)

2 Cost considerations
– affordable, or a money pit?

Parts for the Fiat 500 and 600 are readily available through specialist suppliers. For anyone proposing a major repair or vehicle restoration, the following can be used as a price guide.

Mechanical parts
Engine, new ● x 1000, reconditioned ● x 700, used ● x 300
Cylinder head ● x 150 (500), ● x 250 (600)
Rocker cover ● x 60 (500), ● x 80 (600)
Piston sets ● x 230 (500), ● x 400 (600)
Gearbox, new ● x 500, reconditioned ● x 350, used ● x 200
Driveshaft ● x 50-100 according to the model
Clutch pressure plate ● x 45, friction plate ● x 25, release bearing ● x 23
Clutch (fitted) approx ● x 250
Brake drum ● x 25, shoes (per wheel) ● x 35, master cylinder ● x 18, wheel cylinder ● x 7
Brake light switch ● x 6
Carburettor ● x 150
Fuel pump ● x 20
Air filter ● x 12-20; high performance ● x 80
Steering box ● x 70

Engine removed from a 500R together with doors, seats and other items.
(William Imrè/Bill Wolf)

Electrical
Headlight ● x 25, with sidelight
incorporated ● x 45
Distributor ● x 50-70
Coil ● x 25
Starter motor ● x 50

Suspension and axles
Front leaf spring ● x 70-90
Rear spring ● x 75-100
Shock absorber ● x 20, Koni ● x 100
Replacement front suspension assembly
(complete) ● x 600
Stub axle ● x 65
Wheel bearing ● x 30

Lifting a Fiat 500 bodyshell is a delicate
operation. L-R: William Imre, Bill Wolf and
Mauricio Posso. (Bill Wolf)

Body panels and trim
Front panel (average according to model) ● x 125
Front inner panel ● x 30
Front wing arch ● x 90
Front inner arch ● x 30
Rear wing arch ● x 60
Rear inner arch ● x 30
Rear wing ● x 250 (500), ● x 350 (600)
Arch repair section ● x 25-30
Sills ● x 15-40
Inner sills ● x 15-50
Battery holder ● x 10
Front bonnet ● x 70-100
Floorpan ● x 35-50 (Giardiniera ● x 75)
Floorpan with repair section ● x 40-50
Door ● x 115-150, ● x 350 (500D)
Door handle set ● x 35
Engine cover lid ● x 75-115
Jack support ● x 10
Bumper, front ● x 20-35, rear 25-35 (stainless steel ● x 40)
Fabric sunroof ● x 40, with frame ● x 60, long version ● x 200-275
Exhaust system ● x 70 (not fitted)

Baby Fiats, this is a
500L, enjoy a loyal
following.
(Peter Jones)

Interior
Door card set ● x 40
Door pull ● x 5-10
Window surround ● x 12

3 Living with a Fiat 500 or 600
– will you get along together?

You either love them or are indifferent to them, and if it's the latter you probably won't be reading this! Fiat's babies have so much charisma that it's difficult not to admire their curvaceous lines, cuddly shape, compact engineering and Latin appeal. They might appear fragile owing to their minimal dimensions but, as anyone who has owned or driven an example will confirm, these cars are wonderfully robust.

Despite its small size, the 600 is a practical family saloon. (Fiat)

Good points

The 600 was designed at a time when fuel supplies were restricted and there was a need to economise. It was also devised as a small car but one with the capacity to transport four people in comfort, and have space for their luggage. In achieving this criteria, the designer chose a rear engine layout to allow the maximum amount of interior space to be used for passenger accommodation. Fine tuning of the chassis has meant that the car enjoys tenacious roadholding, something that the motorsport fraternity was quick to realise; thus, the 600 became a familiar sight on the rally scene. The 600 also

Throughout production, the 600 lost some of its austerity: this 600L has a padded facia. (Fiat)

became synonymous with specialist tuners and converters, none more so than Carlo Abarth who took delivery of his first Fiat 600 in 1956.

Though now rarely seen, the 600 inspired the Multipla, the first MPV. Utilising the same wheelbase as the saloon, Fiat adopted a forward-control layout and, retaining the rear drivetrain, produced a versatile six-seater. The middle and rear rows of seats collapsing when needed, allowed the vehicle to be used as a freight carrier.

Smaller than the 600 and with a frugal air-cooled twin-cylinder engine delivering minimal performance, the 500 Nuova is still a common sight in Italy. Demure almost beyond belief, the 500 really is only a 2+2, and yet it is quite common for it to accommodate four adults and luggage in a style only the Italians can achieve. Like the 600, the 500 is remarkably rugged, has amazing handling characteristics, and is able to survive the extremes of Italy's weather and topography.

It is the later cars, the 600D, 500D, 500F, 500L and 500R that have survived in greater numbers. As production progressed so the cars became all the more sophisticated and, in the case of the 500, sported such equipment as a fuel gauge and more comprehensive instrumentation, along with increased comfort and a better quality finish. Later derivatives, such as the 126, were styled to afford greater versatility in respect of interior space and comfort, though arguably at a cost to original charm and personality.

Happily there exists a universal and thriving 500 and 600 community, with virtually all parts for all models being available. In the main, servicing and replacement parts are affordable, with only the most obscure items being harder to source.

The 500 Nuova (in this instance a 500D) captured the essence of the Topolino. (Richard Dredge)

Bad points
Early cars were very basic and had minimal performance. Survival rate of early models is poor, even in their native Italy, and endeavours to restore one of these rarities will be challenging. So basic were the first 500s that they did not even have opening windows, ventilation being mostly supplied through the roll-back fabric roof. Needless to say, the 600, and particularly the 500, are severely restricted when it comes to passenger accommodation, a

characteristic which helps give these cars their cheeky appeal. On the 600 and 500, the fuel tank is positioned at the front of the car under the bonnet, which means that luggage space is strictly limited. Filling the petrol tank is not easy, and requires use of a funnel if spillage is to be avoided.

Driving long distances in these cars is quite feasible, such is their simple yet robust engineering coupled with legendary reliability. What is not so acceptable is the noise from the engine, the narrow seats and cramped accommodation, minimal performance, especially when climbing hills, and the

The Ghia Jolly is one of several variants based on the 500 Nuova.

fact that being surrounded by large vehicles on the open road can be intimidating.

The 126Bis, with its water-cooled twin-cylinder engine, earned a reputation of being unreliable, the cause being excessive engine vibration which could lead to wiring connections and hoses becoming detached. The engine on the 126Bis was always prone to oil spillages and head gaskets failing.

Both the 600 and 500 are vulnerable to corrosion around the front quarters, including the luggage compartment and scuttle, wheelarches, sills and floorpan. The engine compartment cover, too, is vulnerable to rust, as are the rear wheelarches.

Fiat 600s, especially early models, are difficult to source. Late model 600s, such as the basic 600E, can make the basis of a sound purchase. (Fiat)

From 1964, the 600 was produced with front-hinged doors, large headlamps and 767cc engine. Featured is the 'economy' 600E. (Fiat)

Owing to the diversity of models, enthusiasts have particular preferences when considering a vehicle. Early models have appeal for their rarity, but later cars, which to the untrained eye appear similar, are popular because of their level of equipment and ease of acquiring replacement parts. Some models, such as the Multipla, are so rare that they appeal to the connoisseur and are highly collectable.

Late model 500s are the easiest to source. (Peter Jones)

Fiat 600, rare early model	90%
600D	80%
Multipla 600 &600D	100%
500 Nuova Economica (very rare early model)	100%
500 Normale	90%
500D	80%
500F	75%
500L	75%
500R	70%
Giardiniera estate car	90%
126	40%
126Bis	30%
Specialist, eg Abarth (not covered in this book)	100%+

In Abarth guise the 600 is a hot performer. (Peter Jones)

Variants such as the NSU Weinsberg, Jagst, Autobianchi Bianchina, Vignale Gamine, Jolly, Zastava, Coriasco, SEAT and Siata are all sought after by 500/600 aficionados and therefore command values not in keeping with the above.

The 500 Nuova was introduced in 1957. Build quality was initially poor and the specification too spartan. Few original 500s exist. (Fiat)

A rarity is the Multipla which can seat six adults. (Fiat)

The 500-based Gamine, with its dummy radiator, gave the little Fiat an almost droll appearance.

The Giardiniera accommodated four adults, and the sideways-laid engine under the floor ensured maximum carrying capacity. (Richard Dredge)

5 Before you view
– be well informed

To avoid the frustration of a car not meeting your expectations, remember to ask specific questions when you call *before* viewing. Also, check the current values of the model you are interested in in the classic car magazines, which give both a price guide and auction results.

Where is the car?
Is it going to be worth travelling to view the car? A locally advertised car, although it might not sound very interesting, can add to your knowledge for very little effort, so make a visit, it might even be in better condition than expected.

Dealer or private sale?
Establish early on if the car is being sold by its owner or by a trader. A private owner should have all the history. A dealer may have more limited knowledge of a car's history, but should have some documentation. A dealer may offer a warranty/guarantee (ask for a printed copy) and finance.

Cost of collection and delivery?
A dealer may well be used to quoting for delivery by car transporter. A private owner may agree to meet you halfway, but only agree to this after you have seen the car at the vendor's address to validate the documents. You could meet halfway and agree the sale but insist on meeting at the vendor's address for the handover.

View,when and where?
It is always preferable to view at the vendor's home or business premises. In the case of a private sale, the car's documentation should tally with the vendor's name and address. Arrange to view only in daylight and avoid a wet day. Most cars look better in poor light or when wet.

Reason for sale?
Do make it one of the first questions. Why is the car being sold and how long has it been with the current owner? How many previous owners?

Left-hand drive to right-hand drive/specials and convertibles?
If a steering conversion has been done, it can only reduce the value of the vehicle and it may well be that other aspects of the car still reflect the specification for a foreign market. Cars that have been customised or have larger engines fitted must be given special consideration as to the competency of the conversion.

Condition (body/chassis/interior/mechanicals)?
Ask for an honest appraisal of the car's condition. Ask specifically about some of the check items described in chapter 7.

All original specification?
An original equipment car is invariably of higher value than a customised version.

Matching data/legal ownership?

Do VIN/chassis, engine numbers and license plate match the official registration document? Is the owner's name and address recorded in the official registration documents? For those countries that require an annual test of roadworthiness, does the car have a document showing it complies (an MoT certificate in the UK, which can be verified by the DVSA on 0300 123 9000 or online at gov.uk/check-mot-status)?

If a smog/emissions certificate is mandatory, does the car have one? If required, does the car carry a current road fund license/license plate tag?

Does the vendor own the car outright? Money might be owed to a finance company or bank: the car could even be stolen. Several organisations will supply the date on ownership, based on the car's licence plate number, for a fee. Such companies can often also tell you whether the car has been 'written off' by an insurance company. In the UK, these organisations can supply vehicle data:

HPI   0113 222 2010
AA   0800 056 8040
DVLA   0844 453 0118
RAC   0330 159 0364

Other countries will have similar organisations.

Unleaded fuel?

If necessary, has the car been modified to run on unleaded fuel?

Insurance?

Check with your existing insurer before setting out, your current policy might not cover you to drive the car if you do purchase it.

How you can pay

A cheque/check will take several days to clear and the seller may prefer to sell to a cash buyer. However, a banker's draft (a cheque issued by a bank) is as good as cash, but safer, so contact your own bank and become familiar with the formalities that are necessary to obtain one.

Buying at auction?

If the intention is to buy at auction see chapter 10 for further advice.

Professional vehicle check (mechanical examination)

There are often marque/model specialists who will undertake professional examination of a vehicle on your behalf. Owners clubs will be able to put you in touch with such specialists. Other organisations that will carry out a general professional check in the UK are –

AA 0800 056 8040 / www.theaa.com/vehicle-inspection (motoring organisation with vehicle inspectors)
RAC 0330 159 0720 / www.rac.co.uk/buying-a-car/vehicle-inspections (motoring organisation with vehicle inspectors)

Other countries will have similar organisations.

6 Inspection equipment
– these items will really help

Before you rush out of the door, gather together a few items that will help as you work around the car.

This book
This book is designed to be your guide at every step, so take it along and use the check boxes to help you asses each area of the car you're interested in. Don't be afraid to let the seller see you using it.

Glasses (spectacles)
Take your reading glasses if you need them, to read documents and make close-up inspections.

Magnet (not powerful,a fridge magnet is ideal)
A magnet will help you check if the car is full of filler, or has fibreglass panels. Use the magnet to sample bodywork areas all around the car, but be careful not to damage the paintwork. Expect to find a little filler here and there, but not whole panels. There's nothing wrong with fibreglass panels, but a purist might want the car to be as original as possible.

Torch
A torch with fresh batteries will be useful for peering into the wheelarches and under the car.

Probe or small screwdriver
A small screwdriver can be used – with care – as a probe, particularly in the wheelarches and on the underside. With this you should be able to check an area of severe corrosion, but be careful – if it's really bad the screwdriver might go through the metal!

Overalls
Be prepared to get dirty. Take along a pair of overalls if you have them.

Mirror on a stick
Fixing a mirror at an angle on the end of a stick may seem odd, but you'll probably need it to check the condition of the underside of the car. It will also help you to peer into some of the important crevices. You can also use it, together with the torch, along the underside of the sills and on the floor.

Digital camera
If you have the use of a digital camera, take it along so that later you can study some areas of the car more closely. Take a picture of any part of the car that causes you concern, and seek a friend's opinion. Ideally, have a friend or knowledgeable enthusiast accompany you: a second opinion is always valuable.

7 Fifteen minute evaluation
– walk away or stay?

Only buy a vehicle from an individual who can prove that they are the person named in the vehicle's registration document (V5C in the UK) and, preferably, at the address shown in the document. Also check that the VIN or chassis number/frame and engine numbers of the car/motorcycle match the numbers in the registration document.

Main areas of the 600 (illustrated) and 500 bodyshells prone to corrosion are the front compartment, front and rear wheelarches, sills and floorpan. (Fiat)

Exterior and badging

First impressions are important when looking at a 500 or 600. If it is your choice to find a car that is immediately usable and not one that is going to require substantial body repairs or even a complete restoration, you should look carefully at the vehicle as a whole, taking note of the paint condition and any obvious defects, such as damaged bumpers and trim as well as minor dents in the body panels.

Owing to the growing popularity of the Fiat 500, in particular, it is best to be wary about cars that might have been languishing in not-so-perfect conditions for long periods, and then being quickly resurrected for a quick and lucrative sale. What might seem a good purchase can easily result in an expensive mistake. Be suspicious about newly-applied paint, especially if the vendor cannot show the vehicle to have been professionally repaired. By applying a magnet to key areas of the bodywork it is possible to ascertain whether there is filler present.

Start at the front of the vehicle and examine the outer panel. This is an area vulnerable to stone chips and, if there are signs of corrosion here, both above and below the bumper, you will need to open the front compartment to check whether rot has spread to the inner front panel. Even the slightest sign of blistering paint on the outer panel can be indicative of a potentially serious problem. Be aware that damage or corrosion to the Multipla's large front panel will be difficult and expensive to repair.

The shape of the bonnet, and indeed the front profile of the car, makes it

When checking the front compartment, look for rust on the front inner and outer panels, under the spare wheel and around the fuel tank. (Fiat)

vulnerable to minor parking damage, and, therefore, any distortion, signs of accident repair, or even differences in paint colour should be investigated. The bonnets of all models tend to flex, and whilst this is not a problem, it is worth checking the inner section for any obvious signs of damage or rust.

While you have the front bonnet open, it is worth looking around carefully to gauge the general condition. Rust tends to form beneath the battery tray and where the spare wheel is located. On the 126 and 126Bis, water enters the front compartment via the seals around the bonnet and collects in the well accommodating the spare wheel. Still

Rust can form along the bonnet sides and down the seams joining the front panel and wings. (Bill Wolf)

with the front compartment open, take a look at the fuel tank on the 500 and 600 which is susceptible to leakage around the bottom edges. Check, too, the brake fluid reservoir which, with age, can leak fluid.

The top of the front panel where it meets the front bonnet lid, the seams where the front wings join, and the front wheelarches, are areas that are vulnerable to corrosion. Mud and grime, if not regularly removed, build up over the years. On a particularly bad example, the metal will have rotted away to the point where holes in the panels are evident.

Before examining the doors, take a

Wheelarches, door bottoms and sills depict a classic state of disrepair on this late model 500. (Bill Wolf)

look at the valance under the front screen. Rusting at the outer edges is probably due to drain holes becoming blocked.

The doors on all baby Fiats are susceptible to corrosion along the lower edges. This is not because the manufacture or the metal is inferior, but because drain holes become blocked, thus allowing moisture to collect. The design of the doors allows water to drain down the glass and through the holes in the door bottoms. If there is evidence of rust it will be necessary to replace the doors. Open and close the doors in order to check for easy closure, and in the event of discovering that the doors have dropped, suspect that the hinge bushes and pins require renewal. Check for signs of rusting around the quarterlights, which could be a difficult and time-consuming job to make good.

The door sills, both the inner and outer sections, have a propensity to rust, which means that the majority of cars offered for sale will have had replacement sills fitted

Inspect the roof for damage or tears in the fabric; corrosion can set in where the canvas joins the rear bodyshell. (Richard Dredge)

at some time. It is possible to check for outer sill corrosion by examining the vehicle from the outside and looking beneath the car. Lifting the matting on the cabin floor will show if there is evidence of rot. Some owners when selling a car with rotten sills have been known to fit new sills over the rusting units, the result being that within a very short time the corrosion will have spread to the replacement parts.

It is now time to give the roof some attention, which on all models are generally trouble free. With vehicles fitted with a sunroof, it is pertinent to check the structure where the canvas is attached at the rear, as this is the area where corrosion can manifest. The roof opening mechanism should be checked to ensure that it works correctly and that the sunroof material is free from tears or damage.

Looking at the rear quarters of a car, note any obvious signs of rust around the rear wheelarches. Usually any corrosion is restricted to this area and, therefore, if the rear wings are showing signs of corrosion, you should suspect that the vehicle is in a particularly poor condition. Outer wing repair sections can be obtained, a benefit if the vehicle

Rear wheelarches and the engine compartment should be examined closely.

is going to be restored, the only problem being that the repair section does not incorporate the whole arch, and is short of the door sill by approximately four inches. The inner wheelarches are susceptible to rot in the same way as the front wheelarches, ie. where they join on the outer edge, and the inner arches suffering from a build up of mud and grime having been allowed to collect over many years. Take care to closely

The grille above the engine compartment tends to rust on 500s.

examine the inside of the wheelarches; if there is evidence of any kinks in the metal work it could be indicative of the vehicle having been involved in a rear impact.

Engine covers on all air-cooled models are mostly rust-free, though in extreme cases the louvres can corrode. Treating a panel with a rusted grille is not an easy task and it may be profitable in the long term to source a replacement component. On the 500 Nuova, the grille above the engine panel is not available as a replacement item, which means that cars showing signs of rot here should be treated with caution. Giardinieras suffer similar problems to saloons: in extreme cases a Giardiniera's full-height rear door can corrode at the base and at the top where it meets the roof. Giardiniera cooling vents are particularly susceptible to rot, and while checking this area, glance along the car's side windows; corrosion there is difficult to address.

Engine covers fitted to air-cooled 126 models are susceptible to rot, both on the cooling louvres and the lower edge of the hatch. The water-cooled 126Bis has plastic cooling louvres positioned aft of the wheelarches above the swathe line, but check for corrosion where the mouldings fit into the rear quarters. The bottom edge of the full-height tailgate can rust, so look for signs of impending problems here.

A specific area to check is the floor, and there are few 500s and 600s that have not had replacement floors fitted or, at least, repaired. It is comforting to know that replacement floorpans are easy to source and are relatively cheap, so be cautious of a car that shows evidence of a plated floorpan; it is a sign of a false economy measure.

Before examining the underside of the car, it is prudent to check the cabin interior. Rust forming around the drain holes and seat runners and in the footwells will be easy to spot, and if the problem is really serious, there may well be holes in the floor. Even a musty smell coming from within the vehicle and evidence of a damp floor covering should suggest the floorpan to be beyond repair.

Finally, as far as the vehicle's exterior is concerned, check the tyres, wheels, trim and badging. Bumpers, nudge bars, mirrors and brightwork should ideally be damage free. Headlights, direction indicators and rear lamps should be in working order, check the efficiency of the windscreen wipers, ensure that the windscreen is free from chippings and cracks, and that all windows are in good order. Tyres should not show signs of improper wear, ie. the tread is worn evenly, hub caps should be in place and wheels free from damage.

Badging is important as it should positively identify a particular model. The 600 featured a roundel on the front panel flanked by horizontal 'wings' level with the upper extent of the circle, central to it and to its lowest part. Later models, from 1965, were fitted with an angular badge flanked by a single set of wings. Throughout production, cars had a 'Fiat 600' script attached to the right-hand side of the engine cover below the cooling louvres. The 500 Nuova had a simple rounded badge flanked by wings on the front panel and Nuova 500 in script on the bottom left-hand side of the engine cover. In 1968, badging changed to an upright rectangular Fiat badge on the front panel, the last models to be built having an elongated badge. The Giardiniera was fitted with an elaborate frontal badge having a somewhat grille-type appearance.

Interior

All models have fairly basic interiors with metal or metal and plastic facias. There is little in the way of luxury, but seats are comfortable and supportive, even over long distances. Seats are simply upholstered in vinyl and should be clean, stain and

Facia detail is spartan on 500s; only the 500L has more comprehensive instrumentation. (Richard Dredge)

damage free. Door panels and flooring should also be in good condition; a vehicle in a less than acceptable state should be considered carefully as it will inevitably prove costly to refurbish.

The 126 was furnished with cloth upholstery, the Bis model having a folding rear seat which added to the car's interior carrying capacity. Cloth upholstery can wear on the seat edges, but beware of serious wear or sagging front seats. Instrumentation is minimal on all baby Fiats but all controls and switches should operate efficiently.

Should you be fortunate enough to be looking at a 600 Multipla, the interior will appear austere. Three versions of the Multipla were offered, a four/five-seater, six-seater and taxi, the last two mentioned having three rows of seats, the centre and aft folding flat. On all models of 600 and 500, it essential to check that seats move and operate correctly. When considering a variant, such as the Vignale-Fiat Gamine, it is prudent to ensure that interiors and hoods are in good condition, otherwise the car will prove expensive to repair or restore.

Paperwork/ownership/legality
Owing to the fact that so many baby Fiats were built, and that there is a healthy survival rate, it is important to establish that all the necessary paperwork is in order, especially if considering the purchase of an imported vehicle. See chapter 11 for further information.

Mechanicals
The task of examining the mechanical aspect of a vehicle will be dealt with in chapter 9 but it is prudent to state at this stage that the main areas for concern are

the suspension and suspension mountings, kingpins, oil pressure, poor starting, oil leaks, engine cooling, engine and gearbox mountings, and engine dipsticks. Do be aware, especially with the 500, that cars may have been retrospectively fitted with larger engines, those from the air-cooled 126 being favoured.

Opening the engine cover will tell you much about the state of maintenance the owner has bestowed upon the car. A dirty engine compartment with evidence of oil leakage will infer that only minimal servicing has been afforded. The 600 and Multipla being water-cooled, it is necessary to check for evidence of coolant leakage and to ensure the radiator and cooling fan are in good order. Look for oil leaking from the rocker cover on air-cooled models, a sign that the gasket has perished and should be replaced. Unlike 500 saloon models which have vertical engines, those fitted to the Giardiniera are laid flat to allow for an unobstructed load platform. The 126Bis water-cooled engine is also laid on its side and it is not unusual to discover pools of oil on the top surface of the casing. If neglected, the 126Bis engine compartment can appear as a sorry mess.

Do take time to examine the engine compartment bulkheads for signs of damage incurred as a result of a rear impact.

When taking a car for a test drive it doesn't take long to acclimatise with the controls and instrumentation. Unusual on the 600 is the positioning of the choke, which is positioned rear of the gear lever and adjacent to the driver's seat, the starter control being alongside.

The 500 Nuova is all the more basic and only the later models have what might be called comprehensive instrumentation. Getting into a 500 for the first time is a culture shock as the interior feels confined. Starting the engine on a 500 can be tricky, calling for use of the floor-mounted choke lever and under-dash hand throttle when cold, and when warm, cranking the starter and using the accelerator to determined effect when it fires. Most obvious about the 500 is its tardy performance, which means that emerging from a road junction has to be carefully judged. Keeping up with urban traffic is less of a problem but driving on the open road does call for certain techniques, such as running the engine at high revs and not being ambitious about overtaking.

Walk away or stay?
You should now know whether the car you are looking at is worthy of more detailed examination as per chapter 9. If the vehicle is in need of restoration, turn to chapter 13. Should you be in any doubt about the car, it would be prudent to walk away and hope that the next example you view inspires more confidence.

8 Key points
– where to look for problems

When buying a baby Fiat there are six major points to consider:
- External body condition
- Interior of vehicle
- Underbody
- Engine condition
- Road test
- Service history/complete documentation

Owing to the diminutive size of a baby Fiat, it is all too easy to overlook potential problems believing them to be 'insignificant'. Nevertheless, take your time when looking at a car, and as long

Look for signs of rust in the front compartment, on inner and outer front panels and around the wheelarches. (Ian Wallace/Colin Clarke)

Inspect the front transverse leaf spring for rust and check the suspension and steering gear. (Ian Wallace/Colin Clarke)

Engines are reliable but the 500's air-cooled twin can leak oil around the rocker cover gasket. This is how an air-cooled engine should look. (Ian Wallace)

Check the engine bay for signs of rust and evidence of kinks that might indicate the vehicle having been involved in a rear impact. (William Imre/Bill Wolf)

Look for corrosion at the rear of the front wheelarches, along the sills and door bottoms. Rust can also form where the trim is fixed to the body. (Ian Wallace/Colin Clarke)

Fuel tanks have a propensity to rust; check the inner wheelarches, the area beneath the battery and around the brake master cylinder. Rust can form within the well supporting the spare wheel. (Ian Wallace/Colin Clarke)

as an evaluation is made in the order shown at the beginning of the chapter, coming to a decision will be straightforward.

Do not be worried about asking pertinent questions should any aspects of the car concern you; if the vendor cannot supply satisfactory answers, it is probably wise to walk away from the sale.

Unless a purchaser is happy to buy a basket case for the purpose of undertaking a complete restoration, the chosen vehicle, according to budget, should be useable, have an MoT certificate and be of such condition there is no necessity for immediate major repairs. Before agreeing to purchase a vehicle, be confident that the paperwork is in order, and the test drive does not reveal any hidden problems.

9 Serious evaluation
– 60 minutes for years of enjoyment

Circle the Excellent, Good, Average or Poor box of each section as you go along. The totting up procedure is detailed at the end of the chapter. Be realistic in your marking!

Use a weak magnet to check metal for filler.

Early 600s are identified by their wing-top lights. All baby Fiats are prone to corrosion around the front of the car, though this example appears to be in remarkably good condition.
(Steven Abbott)

Exterior

The first sighting of a prospective car will give an indication as to the likely outcome of the evaluation. For the potential buyer who has not seen a 500 or 600 at close quarters, the diminutive size of the cars comes as something of a shock. Owing to the cars' minimal proportions, it is all too easy to incorrectly assume that repairs and restoration will be straightforward and relatively inexpensive. All baby Fiats are prone to corrosion, and a car that has been neglected will more often that not appear as a sorry mess. Both the 600 and 500 suffer from similar problems, and in the case of the 500, the build quality of the earliest examples mean that very few cars have survived. Should the bodyshell on the car that is being inspected show signs of serious corrosion, it is likely that the car is beyond economic restoration.

Paint

Under normal circumstances, the paint on the 500 and 600 wears quite well but it has to be accepted that on vehicles which are, at the youngest, well over thirty years-old and never been subject to a respray, are likely to be a need of attention. On late models, such as the 126 and 126Bis, the paint, if original, will probably have faded. Where vehicles have been repainted, check that there

A vehicle that is offered for sale may have been given an economy respray. Look carefully at the paintwork for defects. (Peter Jones)

is documentary evidence of the work having been carried out by a paint specialist. Look also for signs of any paint problems (see chapter 14) which could suggest a second-rate 'economy' job, especially if there are differences in shade. If evidence exists that the car's colour has changed, make sure the registration documents have been altered accordingly.

Bodywork and panels

	Ex	Gd	Av	Po
	4	3	2	1

Start the tour of the car at the front. Be wary of a newly-painted car, especially if it appears work carried out is superficial. Open the front luggage compartment and ensure that the lid prop keeps the bonnet cover securely in the raised position. The front inner and outer panels are prone to rust, therefore carefully check the outer panel and above and below the bumper, for signs of rust. Paint blisters, caused by stone chippings hitting the surface, suggest that corrosion exists and is breaking through the paint. Examine the area around the headlights, and along the vertical seams, which are beneath the headlights on 600 models, and at the leading edges of the 500's front wings, as it is not uncommon to find decay in these areas. The upper edge of the front panel is also vulnerable to rust, as is the leading edge of the front compartment lid. Check along the shut lines of the bonnet lid for corrosion, something that

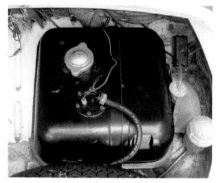

Rusting is evident around the inner wheelarches. Petrol tanks leak with age, as does the brake master cylinder. (Steven Abbott)

is important on the 126 as water collects in the rubber seal. The

bonnet lid tends to flex but should be free from dents and stone chips. Check the inside lip for signs of cracking, and along the edges of the bonnet where the edges meet the inner frame, this being a rust trap.

There's not much space for luggage in the 600D's front compartment. The floor covering is contaminated, and the metal beneath corroded. (Martin Bates)

Now take a close look at the inner panel by first removing the spare wheel, the securing device of which should be in good condition. The well in which the spare wheel is secured tends to hold moisture and if not regularly dried and cleaned will corrode. The inner front panel is also a trap for corrosion and, if severely decayed, can virtually rot through. While examining the front boot area, ensure that the inner wheelarches are secure and rot-free. Check, too, the compartment floor. It should be rust-free, but on all models, including the later generation 126 models, corrosion can set in. Check for leakage from the battery and brake fluid reservoir, and pay attention to the petrol tank which has a tendency to leak from the base. On the Multipla, the battery is located in the engine compartment, and the fuel tank is between the rear seat and engine bulkhead. The fuel tank on the 126 is located mid-car beneath the rear seat.

The Multipla's front panel calls for some careful attention as the large expanse of metal is vulnerable to minor damage caused by stone chippings and parking knocks. Any corrosion or damage will not only be expensive to repair, but parts will be difficult to source. Look for signs of corrosion where the upright nudge bars fasten to the body, and along the vertical seams where the front panels join the door posts.

The front wings and wheelarches are also prone to rot and, in severe cases, the metal will have been completely eaten away. It is necessary to carefully feel around for signs of rust even on cars with wheelarches that look healthy on the surface: if the metal isn't smooth there is the possibility that a recent coat of paint may be hiding something sinister.

Rot attacks the front wings, especially down the seams and around the front wheelarches. (Steven Abbott)

Front wings of the 600 are welded over the inner panels to leave a small joint exposed halfway up the A pillar, which eventually fills with mud and debris sprayed from the front tyres. Even though paste filler was used to protect this area, rusting inevitably takes place behind the wing skin.

Particularly vulnerable on all cars is the lower rear section of the front wheelarch, and it is not unusual to find the area has been plated. As long as repairs have been carried out professionally there is little to worry about, but accept that there will be few vehicles that have not needed repair at some time. One of the main concerns is that over a long time, mud and grime collects where the front wings and inner wheelarches join on the outer edge; gently prodding this area will reveal any potential problem.

It is sensible to now look at the rear wings and wheelarches. Be suspicious of a vehicle with evidence of corrosion at the bottom of the leading edges of the rear arches. If this is the case, there is every likelihood that corrosion is more widespread, extending to the inner sills. If rust is evident in the inner rear wheelarches and flitch panels, check the extent of the corrosion because, if it is very prevalent, the

possibility is that the suspension is in danger of collapse. Problems with the 600 are caused by water getting between the two halves of the rear wheelarch panels and seeping to the sills below, resulting in rusting of the rear beam supporting the swinging arms. Once corrosion has formed a hole, the moisture can escape, allowing the beam to survive.

On all 500s and 600s there is a tendency for rust to appear around the rear wheelarches, for which outer repair sections

Rear wheelarches are prone to rot, the decay spreading to the wings. (Ian Wallace/Colin Clarke)

are available. Be aware that such repair sections do not incorporate the whole arch and fail to meet the door sill by approximately 4 inches. Only a car with serious decay will show rot to have spread to the wing itself. The inner wheelarches rot in much the same way as at the front, and while examining this area, it is important to look for any kinks in the structure that might indicate the vehicle has at some time been involved in a rear impact.

Behind the rear wheels on the 600 there is a sealed panel, and while

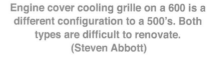

Engine cover cooling grille on a 600 is a different configuration to a 500's. Both types are difficult to renovate. (Steven Abbott)

water can get into this area it is usually evaporated by heat from the engine compartment.

Going to the rear of the car, inspect the engine cover for signs of corrosion around the cooling louvres. The engine compartment cover is not generally a problem area, but if there is rust on the grille, this can be time-consuming and fiddly to rectify.

Finally, if there is evidence of a vehicle having been involved in a frontal impact, there is the possibility that the frame is distorted. It has been known for a vehicle, when having a replacement wing fitted, for the wing assembly not to align with the bodywork.

The upper cooling grille is prone to corrosion on a 500. Note the rusted door bottoms. (Steven Abbott)

Vehicle underside
The floor undersides of all models were usually well-coated with sealant but this does not mean that this area of a car is not

Ex Gd Av Po
[4] [3] [2] [1]

prone to rot. Rusting occurred along the outer edges of the floor where the floorpan, sill stiffener and outer sill are welded. Owing to the vulnerability of a vehicle's underside, most floorpans will have at some time been repaired or replaced, the repair sections being relatively inexpensive and easy to source. Should a car display a patched floorpan, this could signify a 'cheap' temporary repair has been made.

Doors and shut lines

	Ex	Gd	Av	Po
	4	3	2	1

First of all, ensure that the door panels are in good order. Even minor side impacts and parking blemishes look unsightly and can be expensive and difficult to repair, often calling for fitment of replacement doors, either new or used, the latter possibly being in need of repainting prior to installation. The design of the doors allows for any water captured within the door panels to drain away though holes in the door bottoms. All too often these drain holes become blocked with the

Doors and shut lines should be checked. Doors that have dropped need attention to hinges and bushes. (Steven Abbott)

result that the trapped moisture causes rusting. Only close examination of the door bottoms and frames will reveal the existence of corrosion: by feeling around with one's hands it is possible to not only detect decay, but also use of filler. In cases where the doors are badly rusted, the only recourse is to replace them as door repair kits are not generally available.

By looking at the shut lines it will be possible to detect whether a door has dropped, which is often a problem with cars having rear-hinged 'suicide' doors. If this is the case, check the hinges as it possible to replace the pins and bushes.

Rust occurs when water is trapped in door bottoms because of blocked drain holes. (Steve Abbott)

Exterior trim

	Ex	Gd	Av	Po
	4	3	2	1

There is little in way of trim items but what there is tends to become fragile when removed from the vehicle. Make sure mirrors, quarterlights and windscreen bonding are sound, and don't forget to see that the bumpers are intact, have the correct profile and are without dents.

There's little external trim on a baby Fiat. Nevertheless, check bumpers and window surrounds.

One wiper arm on this 500 is missing, the other is bent and without a blade. (Steven Abbott)

Wipers

Ex	Gd	Av	Po
4	3	2	1

These are of single speed on the 500 and 600. Wiper arms should not be bent or damaged, and blades should be in good condition without signs of the rubber fraying. The 126Bis has two-speed wipers, along with a rear screen wiper.

Sunroof

Ex	Gd	Av	Po
4	3	2	1

On models fitted with either a full-length or short sunroof, ensure that the fabric is in good repair. Sunroofs when fitted to early 600s were of the full length variety and fitted over a folding frame; early 500s had a roll-back roof while later cars had a smaller type of opening, again with a folding frame. The hood framework should operate efficiently, and check for signs of corrosion where the fastening clamps attach to the canvas along the rear roof section.

Sills

Ex	Gd	Av	Po
4	3	2	1

The sills on the 600 were originally fitted with alloy strips that were fixed with metal clips, the edges of which are sharp. Rust can often be found where the clip fixes to the bodywork, and once

The sunroof fabric should be in good condition. Check for corrosion where the hood meets the bodywork. (Fiat)

On both the 500 and 600, sills are prone to rusting. New sills are available, but beware of new sills placed over rusted examples to effect 'quick and temporary repairs'. (Steven Abbott)

corrosion has got a hold, water gets inside the sill. Both inner and outer sills are prone to rust on both 500 and 600 models. It is necessary to check from beneath the vehicle, and from inside by lifting the matting, for evidence of problems. It has been known for new sills to be fitted over rusted sills, the result being that the covering sills rot very quickly, thus compounding matters. Where cars have rusted to a great extent, the inner section of the sills behind the doors will need to be replaced.

Jacking points

On early cars particularly, the jacking points were a source of weakness. It has been known when attempting to lift a vehicle for the jacking point to be pushed into the sill.

Ex	Gd	Av	Po
4	3	2	1

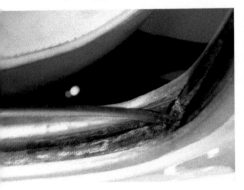

Glass should be intact and the opening mechanism in good working order. Watch for corrosion where the windows drop into the doors. (Steven Abbott)

Glass

Ex	Gd	Av	Po
4	3	2	1

Early examples of the 600 have sliding glasses and these should be easy to open and close. Later models, even before the introduction of the 600D, had winding windows, which again should operate efficiently. With introduction of the 600D, front quarterlights were fitted and it is important that no sign of rust exists. Multiplas have front winding windows, the centre glasses being of the sliding variety. Early 500s did not have opening windows other than the front quarterlights, ventilation being supplied via fresh air collected through small grilles beneath the headlights, and through the opening roof. Within a short time, changes in specification brought about winding windows in the front doors as well as opening quarterlights. All glass should be free from stone chips, scratches and any other visible damage. The Giardiniera has sliding rear windows in addition to wind-down glass and quarterlights in the front doors.

Lights

Ex	Gd	Av	Po
4	3	2	1

Headlight units on the 600 are removed by slackening the lower locking screw located in the bezel, and pulling downwards. Bulbs are retained by spring clips. On the 500, bulbs are accessed from the interior of the luggage compartment. Lenses should be clean and damage free.

As well as checking headlights, pay attention to rear lamps. (Steven Abbott)

It is important to check the tyres, especially when a car has been standing idle for a prolonged period. (Steven Abbott)

Wheels and tyres

Wheel size on the 600 is 3½x12, tyre pressures 17psi front and 23psi rear. Multiplas have the same wheel size as the 600 but tyre pressures are 24psi front and 28psi rear. On the 500, wheel size is 3½x12, tyres 125x12, pressures 17psi front and 23psi rear. The Giardiniera has the same size wheels and tyres as the saloon but pressures are 17psi front and 27-30psi rear according to load. The 126 has 135SRx12 tyres, and the 126Bis has 135/70SRx13 tyres, pressures 20psi front and 25psi rear.

When examining tyres for condition remember that those having split or cracked side walls will result in an MoT failure. A vehicle that has been standing for a long period may well display tyres that have become damaged, and in any event check for uniform wear. Uneven wear could indicate problems with a car's suspension.

Hub bearings and steering joints

Ex [4] Gd [3] Av [2] Po [1]

Ask the vendor to jack the front of the car (unless you are sure of the car's condition, and that the jacking points and jacking mechanism are sound, it is often wise to let the seller undertake such operations). With the wheel clear of the ground, any movement or excess play will become apparent.

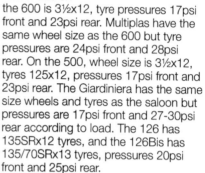

Check for wear in hub bearings and steering joints. Note the debris on the leaf spring. (Steven Abbott)

Interior

Ex [4] Gd [3] Av [2] Po [1]

The interiors on all models can only be described as basic, there being little change to designs throughout production. Characteristic about all baby Fiats is their minimal instrumentation, and it is only the 500L and 126/126Bis that can boast of having anything like a facia console. On the factory-produced Abarth models, such as the 595, it was possible to specify additional instrumentation.

Seats

The seats on the 500 are narrow and look as if they offer only limited support and comfort. While this is true of the

Seats might appear uninviting, but are, nevertheless, supportive. Check for tears in the fabric and signs of sagging. (Richard Dredge)

Multiplas are six-seaters: check that the middle and back row seats fold away. (Tony Spillane)

rear bench, which is designed to accommodate children, the front seats are surprisingly accommodating, even on a long run. Upholstery is a vinyl fabric in colours to contrast with the vehicle's exterior paint colour, that on early 500s being plain material, the 500L having more sumptuous looking pleated seating. It is not uncommon for owners to fit the better quality seats to earlier cars. The front seats have forward

and aft adjustment and additionally tip forwards to allow access to the rear bench. On the earliest 500s, the fixed rear bench was merely a perch intended for children, and when not used for the purpose, doubled as additional luggage space. On later models, the rear seat was redesigned to allow the backrest to fold, thus forming a flat luggage platform.

Seats fitted to the 600 were of fabric material from the outset but market destination and badging can determine provision of vinyl. There is forward/aft adjustment and the seats tip forward to access the rear bench, which can be folded. The Multipla has a folding front passenger seat while those in the centre fold flat to provide a large luggage area. The rear seat also folds to form a luggage base.

Check the condition of a car's front seats; one that sags could be in need of rebuilding or replacement. Cloth seats as fitted to the 600 and 126Bis could show signs of wear to the fabric.

Floorpan
This is dealt with elsewhere but do at least lift the floor covering. In severe

Fiat 500 floorpans do rot. In severe cases, rust holes can be sufficiently large to see the road beneath. (Steven Abbott)

A 600's floorpan rots in much the same way as a 500's; here, part of the floor has been cut away in readiness for renewal. (Martin Bates)

cases of corrosion there will be rot around the drain holes, seat runners and footwells, even to the extent that the road beneath is visible.

Carpets

Rubber matting was used on all models except the 500L, which had carpeting. Ideally, all floor coverings should be intact and free from tears.

Headlining

On vehicles without a sunroof, the headlining is a vinyl material. It should be clean and free from damage.

Door cards

These are of basic quality on the 500 and covered with vinyl to match the colour of a car's interior. On the 600 they are fabric-covered and have small pockets built into the leading edge of the door. Door cards can be easily removed by undoing the retaining screws. The 126Bis has cloth door cards.

Door cards vary with model; on 600s they are usually fabric, and on 500s, vinyl. (Fiat)

Door locks and handles

On cars with 'suicide' doors, the driver's door has an external lock combined with the handle and is located at the leading edge. There is an interior door release with a separate locking device. On models with front-hinged doors, the opening lever (chrome on 600 models) is situated at the leading edge, above the window winder. The Giardiniera's rear door is side-hinged (left-hand side) with the lock on the right-hand side adjacent to the opening.

Window winders

On late 600s and the 600D the winder is a chrome affair, as it is on the 500L, other 500 type models have plastic type winders.

Steering wheel

Two-spoke wheels were standard throughout the range, although some Abarth or Steyr-Puch models have three-spoke

Carpeting and headlining should be free from tears; steering wheels are of the two-spoke variety though some Abarth and Steyr-Puch derivatives have three. (Steven Abbott)

sport wheels. If a car has had the original wheel replaced with a sports type, make sure it does not compromise the appeal of the vehicle.

Handbrake

Ex	Gd	Av	Po
4	3	2	1

On the 600 the handbrake operates on the transmission but on the 500 it acts on the rear wheels.

Boot/trunk interior, spare wheel and tool kit

Ex	Gd	Av	Po
4	3	2	1

Owing to the spare wheel, fuel tank, battery and brake reservoir being located within the front compartment (except Multipla and 126), there is precious little space for luggage. Only the 126/126Bis have any appreciable front compartment luggage space owing to relocation of the fuel tank. The spare wheel fits into a well adjacent to the front panel and is secured by means of a strap. A tool kit containing three spanners, pliers, punch, screwdriver, wheel chock, spark plug wrench, jack and handle was originally supplied. An item to check is the cable-operated bonnet release mechanism. The cable stretches with use and fails at all too frequent intervals. Where a bonnet release mechanism has failed, it is necessary to stand outside the car with one hand pressing on the release button in the cabin, the other hand ready to lift the bonnet manually; not an easy task and made far easier with another pair of hands!

Luggage compartments are configured differently according to model. The spare wheel should be secured with a strap, and there should be a set of tools as supplied with the car. (Fiat)

Mechanicals

Ex	Gd	Av	Po
4	3	2	1

Under the engine cover/hood the 600 and derivatives have water-cooled engines, 500 and derivatives have air-cooled engines. The 126 is air-cooled while the 126Bis is water-cooled.

General impression

Ex	Gd	Av	Po
4	3	2	1

First glance inside the engine compartment reveals how compact the engine and drivetrain is. A dirty and oily compartment will denote lack of care and maintenance. Check the inside of the engine cover for signs of rusting around the grille (see elsewhere in this chapter). The engine bay on both the 500 and 600 is not normally prone to rust, but it is essential to look for kinks in the bulkhead which could indicate that the vehicle has been involved in an accident. If evidence of accident damage exists, there is a need for very careful examination of the driveshafts and transmission system. The immediate concern is the gear lever, which should be upright: if it appears to be at an angle there is every possibility that the gearbox has been moved out of alignment.

Next, examine the driveshafts for correct alignment; it is apparent they are working at an angle, this again is a sign the vehicle has been involved in an impact. The problem here is that whilst the vehicle may appear to drive properly, when it comes to undertaking engine or gearbox repairs calling for removal from the car, it is likely they will not fit when repatriated.

Engine and chassis numbers

Ex Gd Av Po
[4] [3] [2] [1]

On the 600, the identification plate is found either at the top of the engine compartment bulkhead or on the right of the engine compartment wall. The car number is stamped at the top of the engine compartment wall, and the engine number is located on the cylinder block rear wall. On the Multipla, chassis and identification plates are fixed to the engine bulkhead, and the engine number to the crankcase. On the 500, the vehicle identification plate showing car, chassis and engine numbers, is fitted to the scuttle in the front luggage compartment. Additionally, the engine number is fixed to the rear of the engine crankcase.

Engines

Ex Gd Av Po
[4] [3] [2] [1]

These are noted for their robust design and capability of being worked at full speed. The 600's engine is tough but fairly noisy; there is also a degree of tappet noise, and in some instances there can be problems linked to overheating. The radiator fins need regular cleaning as they collect debris and can become sticky, thus blocking the flow of air. It is useful to enquire from the seller whether the oil filter, housed in a centrifugal spinner located at the end of the crankshaft, has been cleaned. Cleaning the filter is a very necessary yet simple operation, but one which is messy and thus often overlooked. The oil filter arrangement is common to both the 600 and 500.

The air-cooled 500 engine is noisy by virtue of its design but is inherently reliable. It is not unusual, though, to see oil leaking from the rocker cover as a result of the rubberised cork gasket material going hard, the remedy being to replace the rocker cover gasket. Should a 500 be difficult to start when the engine is hot, suspect the valve clearance as tappets tend to close, thus reducing clearance tolerances.

The 600's water-cooled engine is compact; note the position of the radiator and fan unit. (Martin Bates)

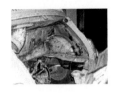

First impressions count when looking at an engine compartment. Check for rust and evidence of accident damage. (Ian Wallace/Colin Clarke)

Three important areas to look at are the dipstick, timing chain and oil pressure. Remove the dipstick – this will tell you much about the condition of the oil – to make sure it is intact. It is not unknown for the end of the dipstick to break off and vanish into the sump, thereby depriving the car owner of knowing how much oil there is in the engine. Timing chains should be changed every 45,000 miles (72,420km) or if noisy. If the oil pressure light stays on when the engine is started, there are two possible causes. In order to avoid a potentially expensive engine rebuild to replace a core plug that has dropped out of the crankshaft, firstly consider fitting a new oil pressure switch.

If the intention is to remove a 500's sparking plugs to check their condition, be aware that the plugs are not easily removed and can easily drop down into the cooling fan cowling.

On 500 saloons the air-cooled vertical twin is easily accessed. On Giardiniera models, the engine is turned on its side and located beneath the luggage platform. (Steven Abbott)

A 500's engine partially stripped. Check that the engine installed is that appropriate to the model, as it is common practice to fit 500s with the 126 power unit. (Steven Abbott)

Another area that often causes concern is the condenser. This is mounted close to the exhaust and in time the cable drops out. This is an all too common problem with 500s, to the extent that most owners carry a spare condenser in the car.

The Giardiniera engine is located beneath the load platform and is turned sideways. The foregoing applies to this model.

If considering a water-cooled 126Bis, it is essential to carefully examine the engine bay which is accessed via the rear hatch. Opening the hatch reveals a lift-up panel beneath which the engine is laid on its side. Owing to configuration of the engine it is susceptible to spraying oil, which has leaked from the dipstick tube, around the compartment. The engine can suffer from excessive vibration, sufficient to loosen hoses and electrical leads.

Many owners will have at some time replaced the car's original engine. Rather than fit like-for-like, in the case of the 500 it is not unusual for a 500R or 126 engine to have been fitted. There is also a possibility that a Fiat Abarth 595 engine has been installed, the benefit being increased torque and acceleration, but only a marginally higher top speed.

Starter cable

Ex	Gd	Av	Po
4	3	2	1

This is a weakness on all 500s as the cable either stretches or becomes crimped. Where a 500 has been fitted with the 126 engine, the problem is non-existent as that engine has a pre-engaged starter.

Transmission

Ex	Gd	Av	Po
4	3	2	1

The gear shift takes some getting used to, especially without synchromesh on 1st gear ratio. Driveshafts on the 500 were weak on the early models but improvements were made on later variants. Sign of gearbox wear is for the vehicle to jump out of gear very easily, this is particularly applicable to the 126 as the thickness of the gears has been reduced to accommodate the synchromesh. Check operation of gear

500 gearbox showing driveshafts.
(William Imre/Bill Wolf)

Driveshafts, rear suspension and hubs on a 500. There is oil contamination around the driveshafts and inner wheelarches. (Steven Abbott)

linkage and rubber couplings between gearbox and selector shaft.

The 600's gearbox can be weak in respect of 2nd gear, sometimes making it difficult to select the ratio.

As with all models there is always the danger that a rear impact has caused damage to the drivetrain, thus selecting gears can be difficult.

Wiring

Ex	Gd	Av	Po
4	3	2	1

Bearing in mind the simplicity of all baby Fiats, wiring is minimal. Nevertheless, care should be taken to inspect for loose or corroded terminals, wiring that has become brittle, and evidence of DIY

Wiring should be checked for overall condition and loose/corroded connections. The rear inner wheelarch of a 600 is shown, complete with body corrosion. (Martin Bates)

accessory installations. The 500L tends to suffer from poor earthing, along with rear lamp units prone to failure.

Radiator and fan

On the 600 and 126Bis check for signs of water and antifreeze leakage. Check, too, the radiator for signs of debris and stickiness which can cause overheating. The 600's radiator has a thermostatically-controlled rod which pushes a cover away as the engine warms up. Check that this is operating correctly and properly connected.

The 500 and derivatives rely on the efficiency of the cooling system for prolonged trouble-free running. The fan and thermostat should be in good condition; a rattling fan is a sign of impending problems, and under-cooling could result in engine seizure.

The condition of a 600's radiator is important. Check that the thermostat is working correctly. When contemplating a 500, check that the fan unit doesn't rattle. (Fiat)

Hoses

There is minimal use of hoses even with water-cooled models. Check all hoses for splits or damage, and ensure all fuel and hydraulic connections are secure.

Battery

Look for signs of leakages and corrosion. On the 500, 600 and 126/126Bis the battery is located in the front luggage compartment; on the Multipla it is positioned above the right-hand side of the engine and is accessed from the rear of the passenger compartment.

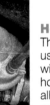

Hoses should not show evidence of splits or wear. (Steven Abbott)

Braking system

Ex Gd Av Po
[4] [3] [2] [1]

Having jacked up each wheel in turn so that it is clear of the ground, there should not be evidence of any of the brakes binding. On the 600, the brake master cylinder is located on the front right-hand side of the vehicle. To access the brake fluid reservoir, lift the mat at the front of the luggage compartment to the right of the spare wheel location; the fluid should be no more or less than 1cm (0.4 inches) from the reservoir brim. Removal of wheels will expose the drum brake shoes and indicate the amount of wear. On the Multipla, the brake master

Drum brake assembly on a 500.
(Steven Abbott)

cylinder is similarly located as to the saloon, access to the reservoir is gained from the passenger compartment by lifting the floor mat.

Clutch master cylinder

This is located at the front of the car. The clutch pedal should have approximately 20mm (¾ inch) free play.

Engine and gearbox mountings

Play in the engine and gearbox mountings is a common problem particularly with the 500 and its derivatives. The mountings are made of rubber and tend to perish, wear being exacerbated by oil contamination. With the engine running, listen for any undue clonking noises.

Fuel pump

Fuel pumps on the 500 are notorious for failure. Attempting to repair a pump is false economy as replacements units are readily available.

Carburettor

Should a carburettor fail, it is easier to fit a replacement unit than try and repair one in situ.

Kingpins

A bone of contention with 500s particularly, the kingpins wear owing to a design fault. Grease does not reach the bottom bushes with the result that an abnormal amount of wear can take place. With each of the front wheels jacked up in turn, rocking of the wheels will reveal the extent of any wear.

Front and rear suspension

The front transverse leaf spring can sag with age and wear causing the front of the car to droop. Should this happen,

Front suspension transverse leaf spring should be concave. On a well used vehicle it is not unusual to find debris collecting between the leaves.
(Ian Wallace/Colin Clarke)

Fiat 500 front suspension.
(Ian Wallace/Colin Clarke)

it will cause an adverse camber angle change and, therefore, uneven tyre wear. Rust has a propensity to build up between the leaves of the spring, the consequence being a poor ride and excessive tyre wear. It has been known, when a transverse leaf spring is worn, for some owners to turn the spring upside down in order to get extra wear from it. When looking at the front suspension the transverse spring should be decidedly concave: treat with suspicion a car with a straight or convex leaf spring. The 600's front suspension, which is similar to that of the 500, is usually somewhat more robust.

The rear suspension is all the more forgiving but it is not impervious to wear. The A frames tend to rust and crack, symptoms usually less common

Front suspension units are durable, but watch out for a worn leaf spring having been turned upside down to get more use from it. (Steven Abbott)

Rear suspension is by coil springs and telescopic shock absorbers.
(Steven Abbott)

on mainland Europe than in the United Kingdom, presumably because of the excessive use of salt on UK roads.
In general, check the suspension mountings, where they are bolted to the body within the front wheelarches, and the rear spring mounting seat at the rear of the car.

Rear suspension showing coil spring and shock absorber, along with rear hub.
(Ian Wallace/Colin Clarke)

Test drive

See chapter 7. A test drive should be a minimum of 15 minutes' duration, during which time check the lightness of steering, the efficiency of the gear selection, suspension and braking efficiency.

Ex Gd Av Po
4 3 2 1

Take a car for a test drive of at least 15 minutes' duration; listen for unusual noises coming from the suspension, brakes, transmission and engine. Steering should be light and precise. (Richard Dredge)

Listen for undue engine, transmission or suspension noises, and watch for signs of the oil pressure and charging indicators lights illuminating, and on the 600 and 126Bis, evidence of over heating.

Ramp check

Ex	Gd	Av	Po
4	3	2	1

Most exhaust or tyre centres will let you put a car on a ramp for a few minutes or so, sometimes for a nominal fee. Start at the front of the vehicle and check for signs of corrosion on the front luggage compartment floor. Check the condition of front transverse leaf spring. Look for wear on the front suspension mountings, signs of rot in the front wheelarches, and condition of sills and door bottoms. Examine the floorpan for condition and quality of repairs, and check the fuel and brake lines. At the rear of the vehicle, look for oil leaks and check alignment of driveshafts, the condition of the exhaust system and evidence of rot in the wheelarches.

Evaluation procedure

Add up the points scored –
176 = excellent, possibly concours;
132 = good/very good; 88 = average;
44 = poor.

To properly examine a car's underside it is necessary to arrange for it to be put on a ramp. Exhaust, sills, floorpan and suspension can then all be viewed easily. (Steven Abbott)

Cars scoring over 123 will be completely usable and will require only maintenance and care to keep in condition. Cars scoring 44 and 89 will need complete restoration, and cars scoring between 90 and 122 will require very careful assessment of necessary repair/restoration costs in order to reach a realistic value.

10 Auctions
– sold! Another way to buy your dream

Auction pros & cons
Pros: Prices will usually be lower than those of dealers or private sellers and you might grab a real bargain on the day. Auctioneers have usually established clear title with the seller. At the venue you can usually examine documentation relating to the vehicle.

Cons: You have to rely on a sketchy catalogue description and history. The opportunity to inspect is limited and you cannot drive the car. Auction cars are often a little below par and may require some work. It's easy to overbid. There will usually be a buyer's premium to pay in addition to the auction hammer price.

Which auction?
Auctions by established auctioneers are advertised in car magazines and on the auction houses' websites. A catalogue, or a simple printed list of the lots for auctions might only be available a day or two ahead, though often lots are listed and pictured on auctioneer' websites much earlier. Contact the auction company to ask if previous auction selling prices are available as this is useful information (details of past sales are often available on websites).

Catalogue,entry fee and payment details
When you purchase the catalogue of the vehicles in the auction, it often acts as a ticket allowing two people to attend the viewing days and auction. Catalogue details tend to be comparatively brief, but will include information such as 'one owner from new, low mileage, full service history', etc. It will also usually show a guide price to give you some idea of what to expect to pay and will tell you what is charged as a 'buyer's premium'. The catalogue will also contain details of acceptable forms of payment. At the fall of a hammer an immediate deposit is usually required, the balance payable within 24 hours. If the plan is to pay cash there may be a cash limit. Some auctions will accept payment by debit card. Sometimes credit or charge cards are acceptable, but will often incur an extra charge. A bank draft or bank transfer will have to be arranged in advance with your bank as well as with the auction house. No car will be released before all payments are cleared. If delays occur in payment transfers then storage costs can accrue.

Buyer's premium
A buyer's premium will be added to the hammer price: don't forget this in your calculations. It is not unusual for there to be a further state tax or local tax on the purchase price and/or on the buyer's premium.

Viewing
In some circumstances it's possible to view on the day, or days before, as well as in the hours prior to, the auction. There are auction officials available who are willing to help out by opening engine and luggage compartments and to allow you to inspect the interior. While the officials may start the engine for you, a test drive is out of the question. Crawling under and around the car as much as you want is permitted, but

you can't suggest that the car you are interested in be jacked up, or attempt to do the job yourself. You can also ask to see any documentation available.

Bidding

Before you take part in the auction, decide on your maximum bid – and stick to it!

It might take a while for the auctioneer to reach the lot you are interested in, so use that time to observe how other bidders behave. When it's the turn of your car, attract the auctioneer's attention and make an early bid. The auctioneer will then look to you for a reaction every time another bid is made, usually the bids will be in fixed increments until the bidding slows, when smaller increments will often be accepted before the hammer falls. If you want to withdraw from the bidding, make sure the auctioneer understands your intentions – a vigorous shake of the head when he or she looks to you for the next bid should do the trick! Assuming that you are the successful bidder, the auctioneer will note your card or paddle number, and from that moment on you will be responsible for the vehicle.

If the car is unsold, either because it failed to reach the reserve or because there was little interest, it may be possible to negotiate with the owner, via the auctioneers, after the sale is over.

Successful bid

There are two more items to think about. How to get the car home and insurance. If you can't drive the car, your own or a hired trailer is one way, another is to have the vehicle shipped using the facilities of a local company. The auction house will also have details of companies specialising in the transfer of cars.

Insurance for immediate cover can usually be purchased on site, but it may be more cost-effective to make arrangements with your own insurance company in advance, and then call to confirm the full details.

eBay and other online auctions

eBay and other online auctions could land you a car at a bargain price, though you'd be foolhardy to bid without examining the car first, something most vendors encourage. A useful feature of eBay is that the geographical location of the car is shown, so you can narrow your choices to those within a realistic radius of home. Be prepared to outbid in the last few moments of the auction. Remember, your bid is binding and that it will be very, very difficult to get restitution in the case of a crooked vendor fleecing you – caveat emptor!

Be aware that some cars offered for sale in online auctions are 'ghost' cars. Don't part any cash without being sure that the vehicle does actually exist and is as described (usually pre-bidding inspection is possible).

Auctioneers

Barrett-Jackson www.barrett-jackson.com, Bonhams www.bonhams.com,
British Car Auctions (BCA) www.bca-europe.com or www.british-car-auctions.co.uk,
Cheffins www.cheffins.co.uk, Christies www.christies.com,
Coys www.coys.co.uk, eBay www.ebay.com or www.ebay.co.uk,
H&H www.classic-auctions.co.uk, RM www.rmauctions.com,
Shannons www.shannons.com.au, Silver www.silverauctions.com

11 Paperwork
– correct documentation is essential!

The paper trail
Classic, collector and prestige cars usually come with a large portfolio of paperwork accumulated and passed on by a succession of proud owners. This documentation represents the real history of the car and from it can be deduced the level of care the car has received, how much it's been used, which specialists have worked on it, and the dates of major repairs and restorations. All of this information will be priceless to you as the new owner, so be very wary of cars with little paperwork to support their claimed history.

Registration documents
All countries/states have some form of registration for private vehicles whether it's like the American 'pink slip' or the British 'log book' systems.

It is essential to check that the registration document is genuine, that it relates to the car in question, and that all the vehicle's details are correctly recorded, including chassis/VIN and engine numbers (if these are shown). If you are buying from the previous owner, his or her name and address will be recorded in the document: this will not be the case if you are buying from a dealer.

In the UK, the current (Euro-aligned) registration document is named "V5C", and is printed in coloured sections of blue, green and pink. The blue section relates to the car specification, the green section has details of the new owner and the pink section is sent to the DVLA in the UK when the car is sold. A small section in yellow deals with selling the car within the motor trade.

In the UK, the DVLA will provide details of earlier keepers of the vehicle upon payment of a small fee, and much can be learned in this way.

If the car has a foreign registration there may be expensive and time-consuming formalities to complete. Do you really want the hassle?

Roadworthiness certificate
Most country/state administrations require that vehicles are regularly tested to prove that they are safe to use on the public highway and do not produce excessive emissions. In the UK, that test (the 'MoT') is carried out at approved testing stations, for a fee. In the USA, the requirement varies, but most states insist on an emissions test every two years as a minimum, while the police are charged with pulling over unsafe-looking vehicles.

In the UK, the test is required on an annual basis once a vehicle becomes three years old. Of particular relevance for older cars, does the certificate issued include the mileage reading at the test date and, therefore, become an independent record of that car's history? Ask the seller if previous certificates are available. Without an MoT the vehicle should be trailored to its new home, unless you insist that a valid MoT is part of the deal. (Not such a bad idea, as at least you will know the car was roadworthy on the day it was tested and you don't need to wait for the old certificate to expire before having the test done.)

Road licence

The administration of every country/state charges some kind of tax for the use of its road system, the actual form of the 'road licence' and, how it is displayed, varying enormously country to country and state to state.

Whatever the form of the road licence, it must relate to the vehicle carrying it, and must be present and valid if the car is to be legally driven on the public highway. The value of the licence will depend on the length of time it will continue to be valid.

Changed legislation in the UK means that the seller of a car must surrender any existing road fund licence, and it is the responsibility of the new owner to re-tax the vehicle at the time of purchase and before the car can be driven on the road. It's therefore vital to see the Vehicle Registration Certificate (V5C) at the time of purchase, and to have access to the New Keeper Supplement (V5C/2), allowing the buyer to obtain road tax immediately.

If the car is untaxed because it has not been used for a period of time, the owner has to inform the licensing authorities, otherwise the vehicle's date-related registration number will be lost and there will be a painful amount of paperwork to get it re-registered."

Certificates of authenticity

For many makes of collectible car it is possible to get a certificate proving the age and authenticity (e.g. engine and chassis numbers, paint colour and trim) of a particular vehicle, these are sometimes called 'Heritage Certificates' and if the car comes with one of these it is a definite bonus. If you want to obtain one, the relevant owners club is the best starting point.

If the car has been used in European classic car rallies it may have a FIVA (Federation Internationale des Vehicules Anciens) certificate. The so-called 'FIVA Passport', or 'FIVA Vehicle Identity Card', enables organisers and participants to recognise whether or not a particular vehicle is suitable for individual events. If you want to obtain such a certificate, go to www.fbhvc.co.uk or www.fiva.org; there will be similar organisations in other countries too.

Valuation certificate

Hopefully, the vendor will have a recent valuation certificate, or letter signed by a recognised expert stating how much he, or she, believes the particular car to be worth (such documents, together with photos, are usually needed to get 'agreed value' insurance). Generally such documents should only act as confirmation of your own assessment of the car rather than a guarantee of value as the expert has probably not seen the car in the flesh. The easiest way to find out how to obtain a formal valuation is to contact the owners club.

Service history

Often these cars will have been serviced at home by enthusiastic (and hopefully capable) owners for a good number of years. Nevertheless, try to obtain as much service history and other paperwork pertaining to the car as you can. Naturally, dealer stamps, or specialist garage receipts score most points in the value stakes. However, anything helps in the great authenticity game, items like the original bill of sale, handbook, parts invoices and repair bills all add to the story and the character of the car. Even a brochure correct to the year of the car's manufacture is a useful document and something that you could well have to search hard to locate in future years. If the seller claims that the car has been restored, then expect receipts and other evidence from a specialist restorer.

If the seller claims to have carried out regular servicing, ask what work was completed, when, and seek some evidence of it being carried out. Your assessment of the car's overall condition should tell you whether the seller's claims are genuine.

Restoration photographs

If the seller tells you that the car has been restored, then expect to be shown a series of photographs taken while the restoration was under way. Pictures taken at various stages, and from various angles, should help you gauge the thoroughness of the work. If you buy the car, ask if you can have all the photographs as they form an important part of the vehicle's history. It's surprising how many sellers are happy to part with their cars and accept your cash, but want to hang on to their photographs! In the latter event, you may be able to persuade the vendor to get a set of copies made.

The minimalism of the 500's interior is all part of the car's character.
(Jamie Wright/Helen Reynolds)

12 What's it worth to you?
– let your head rule your heart!

Condition

If you used the marking system in chapter 9, you'll know whether the car is in Excellent (maybe Concours), Good, Average or Poor condition or, perhaps, somewhere in-between these categories.

Many classic/collector car magazines run a regular price guide. If you haven't bought the latest editions, do so now and compare their suggested values for the model you are thinking of buying: also look at the auction prices they're reporting. Values have been fairly stable for some time now, but some models will always be more sought-after than others. The values published in the magazines tend to vary from one magazine to another, as do their scales of condition, so read carefully the guidance notes they provide. Bear in mind that a car that is truly a recent show winner could be worth more than the highest scale published. Assuming that the car you have in mind is not in show/concours condition, then relate the level of condition that you judge the car to be in with the appropriate guide price. How does the figure compare with the asking price? Before you start haggling with the seller, consider what effect any variation from standard specification might have on the car's value.

If you are buying from a dealer, there will be a dealer's premium on the price.

Desirable options/extras

Few optional extras were offered with the 500 and 600 saloons. Sunroofs were standard on the 600 when introduced but on some derivatives, e.g. SEAT, this was not available. The six-seater 600 Multipla is especially desirable as the seats fold to form a bed or luggage platform. The 500 Giardiniera is also desirable as it offers greater accommodation than the saloon. The 500L has more comprehensive instrumentation but at a cost to the charming originality of the 500D and 500F. The 500, owing to its air-cooling, requires less maintenance than the larger water-cooled 600. The 500R is nearly identical to the 500F but has the 594cc engine that was fitted to the 126, albeit de-tuned to provide 18bhp instead of 23bhp.

Undesirable features

Beware of cars that have been customised. If originality is the key issue, be warned that a number of 500s have been retrospectively fitted with either the 18bhp 594cc engine fitted to the 500R, or the 126's 23bhp 594cc unit. The modifications are most likely to have been made to give the 500 improved performance for use in modern traffic conditions. Some cars, both 600 and 500, have been customised to look like an Abarth conversion, but without that car's stunning performance and characteristics.

Striking a deal

Negotiate on the basis of your condition assessment, mileage, and fault rectification cost. Also take into account the car's specification. Be realistic about the value, but don't be completely intractable: a small compromise on the part of the vendor or buyer will often facilitate a deal at little real cost.

13 Do you really want to restore?
– it'll take longer and cost more than you think

Attempting a 'basket case' restoration might initially be tempting. To see the project through requires much commitment, however.

Having the right working environment is important when restoring a vehicle.
(Ian Wallace/ Colin Clarke)

Taking on a restoration project isn't everyone's choice, especially if the potential owner doesn't have technical acumen. It isn't just mechanical skills that are required: to fulfil a competent restoration, one has to have patience, be able to work methodically to a schedule and, not least, have a sufficiently sized garage or workshop where it is possible to move unheeded around the vehicle in order to make the project viable. Important aspects of any restoration project are having the space in which to strip down the vehicle, somewhere to store the parts, and provision of a workbench on which to clean and renovate those items that can be salvaged for later use.

It is not uncommon for someone who has acquired a vehicle in need of restoration to realise that the task of

Removing, cleaning, renovating and storing parts until required calls for methodical working practice.
(Ian Wallace/ Colin Clarke)

returning it to pristine condition is far more complex, expensive and time-consuming than originally perceived. If this is the case, interest in the project will ultimately be lost, as will the initial investment, especially if a considerable outlay has been made in respect of new or recycled parts, and there is the risk that the unfinished project will be difficult to sell.

Before embarking upon restoration it is wise to familiarise yourself with the car's engineering and construction. The acquisition of a workshop manual is essential, and make sure that you have access to any special tools that may be required. It is possible that a number of replacement panels and components will be needed, in which case carry out a survey of the availability and likely cost involved. Likewise, when budgeting the overall costing of a restoration project, it is vital to allow for unforeseen expenses – they're sure to arise! Don't forget that in the case of certain models, for example the Multipla, Giardiniera and some of the more rare derivatives, body panels can be very difficult to source.

The bodywork will need careful and expert preparation before repainting, and certain other aspects of restoration are likely to be entrusted to specialist craftsmen, such as upholstery and electrics. It is necessary to consider what degree of restoration you are going to be happy with. Can you live with fitting used and recycled parts, or will you be satisfied with nothing less than sheer perfection?

Retaining originality in a restoration project is fine, but do ask yourself if there is a need to update the vehicle in order to make it more usable in modern day traffic conditions. Before you go out to purchase a basket case car, or one that is in such condition that conservation rather than renovation really isn't a practical proposition, do consider whether spending more money on a vehicle that is in first class or usable condition might be more economical in the long run.

Still want to restore? Buying the worst example of the car you want isn't necessarily a bad idea. (Daniel Hammond)

14 Paint problems
– bad complexion, including dimples, pimples and bubbles

Paint faults generally occur due to lack of protection/maintenance, or to poor preparation prior to a respray or touch-up. Some of the following conditions may be present in the car you're looking at.

Give your vehicle the best paint job you can afford. The paint quality complements a vehicle's overall condition. (Haymarket)

Orange peel
This appears as an uneven paint surface, similar to the appearance of the skin of an orange. The fault is caused by the failure of atomised paint droplets to flow into each other when they hit the surface. It's sometimes possible to rub out the effect with proprietary paint cutting/rubbing compound or very fine grades of abrasive paper. A respray may be necessary in severe cases. Consult a bodywork repairer/paint shop for advice.

Metallic paint can look attractive on a car but beware of sealing lacquer becoming damaged and peeling. (Peter Jones)

Cracking
Severe cases are likely to have been caused by too heavy an application of paint (or filler beneath the paint). Also, insufficient stirring of the paint before application can lead to the components being improperly mixed, and cracking can result. Incompatibility with the paint already on the panel can have a similar effect. To rectify it is necessary to rub down to a smooth, sound finish before respraying the problem area.

Crazing
Sometimes the paint takes on a crazed rather than a cracked appearance when the problems mentioned under 'cracking' are present. This problem can also be caused by a reaction between the underlying surface and the paint. Paint removal and respraying the problem area is usually the only solution.

Before a full respray it is necessary to ensure the car's surface is properly prepared. (Ian Wallace/ Colin Clarke)

Blistering
Almost always caused by corrosion of the metal beneath the paint. Usually perforation will be found in the metal, and the damage will usually be worse than that suggested by the area

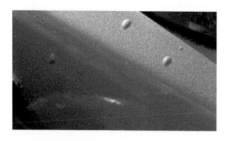

Blistering paint can denote corrosion of the metal beneath. Always examine a car to see whether paint removal is necessary.
(William Imre/Bill Wolf)

Red colours are prone to fading and therefore need polish protection, especially in parts of the world where there is strong sunlight. (Steven Abbott)

Dimples

Dimples in the paintwork are caused by the residue of polish (particularly silicone types) not being removed properly before respraying. Paint removal and repainting is the only solution.

Dents

Small dents are usually easily cured by

of blistering. The metal will have to be repaired before repainting.

Micro blistering

Usually the result of an economy respray where inadequate heating has allowed moisture to settle on the vehicle before spraying. Consult a paint specialist, but damaged paint will have to be removed before partial or full respraying. Can also be caused by car covers that don't 'breathe'.

Fading

Some colours, especially reds, are prone to fading if subject to strong sunlight for long periods without the benefit of polish protection. Sometimes, proprietary paint restorers and/or paint cutting/rubbing compounds will retrieve the situation. Often a respray is the only real solution.

Peeling

Often a problem with metallic paintwork when the sealing lacquer becomes damaged and begins to peel off. Poorly applied paint may also peel. The remedy is to strip and start again.

Minor dents can often be rectified as long as the paint surface is not damaged.
(Maria Cairnie)

the 'Dentmaster', or equivalent process, that sucks or pushes out the dent (as long as the paint surface is still intact). Companies offering dent removal services usually come to your home: consult your telephone directory or the internet.

15 Problems due to lack of use
– just like their owners, baby Fiats need exercise!

Cars that have been stored for a period of time can suffer from a number of problems, not least damaged tyres and faded paintwork. (Steven Abbott)

Cars, like humans, are at their most efficient if they exercise regularly. A run of at least ten miles, once a week, is recommended for classics.

Seized components

Pistons in callipers, slave and master cylinders can seize. The clutch may seize if the plate becomes stuck to the flywheel because of corrosion. Handbrakes/parking brakes can seize if the cables and linkages rust. Pistons can seize in the bores due to corrosion.

Seized components, corroded electrical connections and leaking hydraulics are all signs of an underused car. (Steven Abbott)

Fluids

Old, acidic oil can corrode bearings.

Uninhibited coolant (600 model types) can corrode internal waterways. Lack of antifreeze (again appertaining to 600 model types) can cause core plugs to be pushed out, even cracks in the block or head. Silt settling and solidifying can cause overheating. Brake fluid absorbs water from the atmosphere and should be renewed every two years. Old fluid with a high water content can cause corrosion and piston/callipers to seize (freeze) and can cause brake failure when the water turns to vapour near hot braking components.

Tyre problems

Tyres that have had the weight of the car on them in a single position for some time will develop flat spots, resulting in some (usually temporary) vibration. The tyre walls may have cracks or (blister-type) bulges, meaning new tyres are needed.

Shock absorbers/dampers

With lack of use, the dampers will lose their elasticity or even seize. Creaking, groaning and stiff suspension are signs of this problem.

Rubber and plastic

Radiator hoses on 600 model types may have perished and split, possibly resulting in the loss of all coolant. Window and door seals can harden and leak. Gaiters/boots can crack. Wiper blades will harden.

Electrics

The battery will be of little use if it has not been charged for many months.

The interior of an underused or stored car can deteriorate surprisingly quickly.

Earthing/grounding problems are common when the connections have corroded. Old bullet and spade type electrical connectors commonly rust/corrode and will need disconnecting, cleaning and protection (eg. Vaseline). Sparkplug electrodes will often have corroded in an unused engine. Wiring insulation can harden and fail.

Rotting exhaust system

Exhaust gas contains a high water content so exhaust systems corrode very quickly from the inside when the car is not used.

16 The Community
– key people, organisations and companies in the Fiat world

The mere mention of Fiat kindles in the mind not sports or luxury cars but the diminutive vehicles that are the trade mark of Italy. No film with an Italian flavour would be complete without sightings of little Fiats going about their business, their miniscule size quite academic when it comes to the number of people that can be squeezed into their confines, on the steepness of mountain roads the vehicles can climb. Without their familiar and lovable little cars, towns and cities throughout Italy would be missing an essential ingredient.

In excess of six million 600s and 500s produced over a twenty year period, and thirty seven if the 126 is to be included, can only mean that the Fiat community is, universally, particularly vibrant. Now that both the 600 and 500 have passed their fiftieth anniversaries and Fiat have introduced an all-new 500 that captures the very essence of the vehicle that made its debut in 1957, interest in these wonderfully charismatic cars can only perpetuate.

The Fiat 500 and 600 community is universal. Enthusiast clubs can be found throughout the United Kingdom, Europe, USA, South America, Asia, the Indian sub-continent, South Africa, Australia and New Zealand. There can be hardly a corner of the world that the baby Fiat hasn't ventured. With enthusiasts' clubs come specialists who, as well as being able to procure even the most obscure part, new or previously used, are able to offer repair and restoration services.

The 500 and 600 community includes the legendary Abarth models, those high-performance Scorpion-badged vehicles which have transformed very modestly-powered little Fiats into full-bloodied racing machines. The community extends to the Fiat 500 and 600 variants, such as Autobianchi, Coriasco, Jagst, NSU, SEAT, Siata, Steyr-Puch and Zastava, not to mention the range of Jolly 'beach buggy' vehicles produced by Ghia.

Clubs and specialists

Fiat 500 Club
PO Box 798, Aylesbury, HP22 9DL (UK)
www.fiat500club.org.uk

Fiat Motor Club
www.fiatmotorclubgb.com

Italian Car Club UK (check internet for current contact details)

For listings and contact details of Fiat clubs worldwide log on to www.fiat.com
Fiat UK, www.fiat.co.uk

Middle Barton Garage
55 North Street, Middle Barton, Oxon, tel: 01869 340289, fax: 01869 340110

http://www.middlebartongarage.com
carsandparts@middlebartongarage.com

Ricambio
158 High Street, Banstead, Surrey, SM7 7NZ, tel: 0208 642 8577
http://www.ricambio.co.uk

ItalCorsa
tel/fax: 01252 61335
italcorsa@totalise.co.uk

R. Proietti Ltd
2 Blundell Street, London N7 9BJ, tel: 0207 6070798, fax: 0207 619 0001
www.fiat500.cc

Technoitalia UK
4 Canterbury Court, Battlefield Road, St
Albans, Herts, AL 1 4DX,
tel/fax: 01727 842344
euroitalia500@libero.it

Fiat 500 Ricambi
Wester Thienweh 9, Oostrum (Venray),
Netherlands,
tel: 0031 478 560009
fax: 0031 478 514246

www.fiat500ricambi.com

For specialists and parts suppliers
worldwide, consult an appropriate Fiat
club or the internet.

Whilst many enthusiasts' clubs
publish their dedicated journals or
newsletters, AutoItalia magazine is a
magazine specialising in Italian cars (for
details www.auto-italia.co.uk).

The Fiat Community is worldwide. (Steven Abbott)

17 Vital statistics
– essential data at your fingertips

Production figures

Model	Number built	Build dates
600 Saloon	891,107	1955-1960
600D Saloon	1,561,000	1960-1969
Multipla	76,871	1956-1960
Multipla 600D	83,389	1960-1966
Total	**2,612,367**	
500 Nuova	181,036	1957-1960
500D	640,520	1960-1965
500F&L	2,272,092	1965-1972
500R	334,000	1972-1975
Total	**3,427,648**	
126	80,868	1973-1992
Total	**6,120,883**	

Fiat 600

Engine type: 100.000, rear-mounted, four-cylinder, in-line, 633cc, 60mm bore x 56mm stroke, compression ratio 7.5:1. Maximum power 22bhp at 4600rpm.
Cooling: water, radiator capacity 7.5 pints (4.3 litres).
Fuel tank capacity: 5.9 gallons (27 litres).
Transmission: rear drive, gearbox & final drive combined, four-speeds & reverse, synchromesh on 2nd, 3rd & 4th. Single dry plate clutch.
Suspension: independent front & rear with telescopic shock absorbers, wishbones & transverse leaf at front, semi-trailing arms and coil springs at rear.
Brakes: drums, hydraulic on all wheels, handbrake works on transmission.
Tyres: 5.20x12
Steering: worm & sector, 28.5ft (8.7m) turning circle.
Electrical: 12V, 180w dynamo, 28a/h battery
Dimensions – refer also to chapter 1: wheelbase 6.56ft (2000mm); track, front 3.75ft (1144mm), rear 3.79ft (1154mm); height 4.61ft (1405mm); ground clearance 6.29in (160mm).
Weight: 1289lbs (585kg) unladen, 1972lbs (895kg) laden.
Performance: maximum speed 62mph (100kph), average fuel consumption 49mpg (5.7lts/100km).

600D (where different to the 600)

Engine type: 100D.000, 767cc, 62mm bore x 63.5mm stroke. Maximum power 29bhp at 4800rpm.
Cooling: radiator capacity, 8 pints (4.5 litres)
Dimensions – refer also to chapter 1: track, front 3.77ft (1150mm), rear 3.81ft (1160mm); ground clearance 5.71ins (145mm).
Weight: 1333lbs (605kg) unladen, 2038lbs (925kg) laden.
Performance: maximum speed 68mph (110kph), average fuel consumption 48mpg (5.8 litres/100km).

600 Multipla (where different to the 600)

Engine type: 100.000. Maximum power 21bhp at 4600rpm.
Cooling: radiator capacity, 10.5 pints (6 litres)
Fuel tank capacity: 6.5 gallons (30 litres)
Suspension: coil & wishbone with anti-roll bar at front, coil springs with diagonal swinging arms at rear.
Dimensions – refer also to chapter 1: track, front 4.04ft (1230mm), rear 3.80ft (1157mm); height 5.18ft (1580mm); ground clearance 6.30in (160mm)
Weight: 1610lbs (730kg) unladen, 1959lbs (889kg) laden.
Performance: maximum speed 57.1mph (91.36kph), average fuel consumption 38.5mpg (7.5 litres/100km).

600D Multipla (where different to the 600 Multipla)

Engine type: 100D.008, 767cc, 62mm bore x 63.5mm stroke. Maximum power 29bhp at 4800rpm.
Cooling: 12 pints (6.7 litres)
Steering: turning circle 28ft 10ins (8.80m)
Electrical: 230w dynamo, 36a/h battery
Weight: 1289lbs (585kg) unladen, 1972lbs (895kg) laden
Performance: maximum speed 65mph (105kph), average fuel consumption 33mpg (9 litres/100km).

500 Nuova

Engine: air-cooling, two-cylinder, in-line, ohv, 479cc, type110.000, 66mm bore x70mm stroke, compression ratio 6.55:1. Maximum power 13bhp at 4000rpm.
Sport version: 499.5cc, 21bhp.
Fuel tank capacity: 4.6 gallons (21 litres).
Transmission: rear drive, gearbox and final drive combined, constant mesh on 2nd, 3rd & 4th.
Suspension: independent all-round with telescopic shock absorbers, wishbones & transverse leaf spring at front, semi trailing arms and coil springs at rear.
Brakes: drums, hydraulic all round, handbrake on rear wheels.
Tyres: 125x12
Steering: worm & sector, 28ft (8.6m) turning circle.
Electrical: 12V, 180w dynamo, 32 a/h battery
Dimensions – refer also to chapter 1: wheelbase 6.04ft (1840mm); track, front 3.68ft (1121mm), rear 3.72ft (1135mm); height 4.35ft (1325mm); ground clearance 5.11ins (130mm).
Weight: 1035lbs (470kg) unladen,1498lbs (680kg) laden
Performance: maximum speed 53mph (85kph), average fuel consumption 65mpg (4.5 litres/100km). Sport version: maximum speed 65mph (105kph), average fuel consumption 58mpg (4.8 litres/100km).

500D Nuova (where different to the 500 Nuova)

Engine type: 110D.000, 499.5cc, 67.4mm bore x 70mm stroke, compression ratio 7.1:1. Maximum power 17.5bhp at 4000rpm.
Electrical: 230w dynamo
Dimensions: ground clearance 4.92ins (125mm)

Weight: 1102lbs (500kg) unladen, 1807lbs (820kg) laden.
Performance: maximum speed 59mph (95kph), average fuel consumption 58mpg (4.8 litres/100km).

500 Giardiniera (where different to the 500D)
Engine type: 120.000. Maximum power 17.5bhp at 4600rpm.
Dimensions – refer also to chapter 1: wheelbase 6.36ft (1940mm); rear track 3.71ft (1131mm); height 4.44ft (1354mm); ground clearance 5.31ins (135mm).
Weight: 1223lbs (555kg) unladen, 1928lbs (875kg) laden.
Performance: maximum speed 59mph (95pkh), average fuel consumption 54mpg (5.2 litres/100km).

500F & 500L (where different to 500D)
Engine type: 110F.000. Maximum power 22bhp at 4400rpm.
Fuel tank capacity: 4.75 gallons (22 litres)
Dimensions – refer also to chapter 1: height 4.38ft (1335mm); ground clearance 4.92ins (125mm).
Weight: 1146lbs (520kg) unladen, 1851lbs (840kg) laden
Performance: maximum speed 59mph (95kph), average fuel consumption 51mpg (5.5 litres/100km), 500L fuel consumption 53mpg (5.3 litres/100km).

500R (where different to 500D, 500F & 500L)
Engine type: 126A.000, 594cc. Maximum power 18bhp.
Performance: maximum speed 62mph (100kph).

126
Engine: air cooling, rear-mounted, air-cooled twin, 594cc, type 126A.000, 73.5mm bore x 70mm stroke, compression ratio 7.5:1. Maximum power 23bhp at 4800rpm.
Fuel tank capacity: 4.5 gallons (21 litres).
Transmission: rear drive, swing axle with half shafts, four-speed & reverse with synchromesh on 2nd, 3rd & top. Single dry plate clutch.
Suspension: Independent all round with telescopic shock absorbers, wishbones and transverse leaf spring at front, semi trailing arms and coil springs at rear.
Brakes: drums; hydraulic all round, parking brake acting on rear wheels.
Tyres: 135SRx12.
Steering: worm and helical section.
Electrical: 12V, 230w dynamo, 34a/h battery.
Dimensions – refer also to chapter 1: wheelbase 6.04ft (1840mm); track, front 3.74ft (1140mm), rear 3.95ft (1203mm); height 4.38ft (1335mm); ground clearance 5.51ins (140mm).
Weight: 1270lbs (580kg) unladen, 1984lbs (900kg) laden.
Performance: maximum speed 65mph (105kph), average fuel consumption 54mpg (5.2 litres/100km).

126Bis
Engine type: 126A2.000, rear-mounted, twin-cylinder, in-line, 704cc, water-cooled. 80mm bore x 70mm stroke, compression ratio 8.6:1. Maximum power 26bhp at 4500rpm. Twin-choke carburettor.

Radiator capacity: 6 pints (3.41 litres)
Fuel tank capacity: 4.63 gallons (21 litres).
Transmission: rear drive, four-speed & reverse. Single dry plate clutch.
Suspension: independent all round with telescopic shock absorbers, transverse arms and leaf spring at front, transverse arms and coil springs at rear.
Brakes: drums, hydraulic all round, parking brake acting on rear wheels.
Tyres: 135/70 SR13.
Steering: rack & pinion, 28.2ft turning circle (8.6m)
Electrical: 12V 45A alternator, 34a/h battery.
Dimensions – refer also to chapter 1: wheelbase 6.04ft (1840mm); track, front 3.72ft (1134mm), rear 3.84ft (1169mm); height 4.41ft (1343mm); ground clearance 5.51ins (140mm).
Weight: 1366lbs (620kg) unladen, 1531lbs (695kg) laden.
Performance: maximum speed 72mph (116kph), average fuel consumption 55.64mpg (5.1 litres/100km).

Major specification changes

600: introduced in 1955 to replace the Topolino 500C, 633cc, rear-mounted, water-cooled engine. Forward-control Multipla launched in January 1956.
500 Nuova: launched July 1957.
500 Sport: appeared in August 1958, same specification as Nuova but without sunroof. Sport 'Sunroof' model became available.
500 Giardiniera estate car: appeared in May 1960, production transferred to Autobianchi in spring 1968.
600D and Multipla 600D: models launched in autumn 1960, 767cc engines.
500D: introduced August 1960.
500F: made its debut in March 1965, features include half canvas sunroof and front-hinged doors.
500L: introduced as luxury alternative to 500F.
500R (Replica): launched in 1972, similar to 500F but with 126 air-cooled engine.
126: made its debut in 1972; similar proportions to 500 but angular design and 594cc engine that was fitted to 500R.
126: 650 introduced in 1976 with 652cc; 1983 saw production transferred to Poland.
126Bis: launched in September 1987 as a hatchback, with a 704cc, water-cooled, twin-cylinder engine.

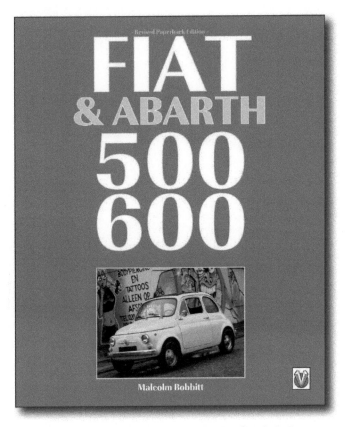

Fiat in Motorsport since 1899
– Anthony Bagnall

ISBN: 978-1-787111-85-1
Hardback • 25x25cm • 160 pages • 195 colour and b&w pictures

A record of Fiat's achievements from the earliest days of racing, including land speed record attempts, the development of 'Balilla' based sports cars, Fiat based specials and the superb 8V coupé of 1952. Abarth's role in achieving three World Rally Championships is also detailed.

For more details call +44 01305 260068, visit www.veloce.co.uk or email info@veloce.co.uk

Index

Abarth, Carlo 10
Abarth 12
Auctions 15, 42, 43
Autobianchi 12

Badging 20
Battery 38
Bianchina 12
Bodyshell 17, 24-27
Bodyshell corrosion 17, 24-27
Bonnet 18, 25
Boot 34
Brake master cylinder 17, 33
Braking system 34, 39, 52, 53

Carburettor 39
Carpets 33
Chassis numbers 15, 35
Cinquecento 3
Clutch 39, 52
Cooling system 38, 53
Corriasco 12
Cost of replacement parts 8

Dimensions 6, 56-59
Doors 18, 28, 33

Electrical 37, 38, 53
Engine 11, 21-23, 35-37, 39
Engine numbers 13, 35
Enthusiasts' clubs & specialists 54, 55
Exterior trim 28

Fiat community 54, 55

Fiat specialists 54, 55
Floorpan 11, 27, 28, 32, 33
Fuel pump 39
Fuel tank 11, 17, 23, 26

Gamine 11, 12
Ghia Jolly 11, 12
Giacosa, Dante 3
Giardiniera 13, 36
Glass 30

Interior 6, 20, 21, 31-35

Headlining 33
Hub bearings 33

Jacking points 30
Jagst 12

Kingpins 39

Lighting 24, 30

NSU Weinsberg 12

Oils 52, 53

Paint & paintwork 24, 25, 50, 51
Paperwork 44-46
Production figures 56
Professional vehicle checks 15

Radiator (see also cooling system) 38
Ramp check 41
Replacement parts 8
Restoration 48, 49, 53

Roof 19, 29
Running costs 6

Scuttle 11
SEAT 12
Seats 31-33
Siata 12
Sills 11, 18, 19, 29
Starter 37
Starter cable 37
Steering 23, 31, 33, 34, 39
Sunroof (see also roof) 29
Suspension 23, 39, 40, 53

Test drive 40, 41
Tool kit 34
Transmission 37
Tyres (see also wheels) 20, 31, 34, 53

Underside 27, 28

Vehicle specifications 56-59
Viewing a vehicle 14-16
Vignale 12

Wheels (see also tyres) 23, 31, 34
Wheelarches 11, 18, 19, 23-26
Windows & window winders 30, 33
Windscreen wipers 29
Wings 11, 18, 19, 26, 27

Zastava 12